# TRAINS

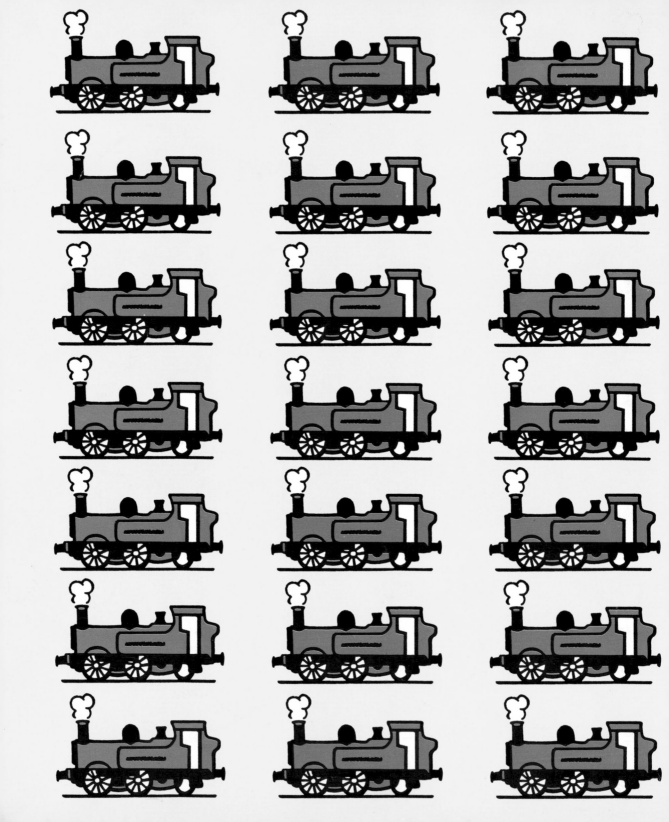

Franklin Watts
95 Madison Avenue
New York, NY 10016

Library of Congress Cataloging-in-Publication Data

Richardson, Joy.
   Trains / by Joy Richardson.
      p.  cm. – (Picture science)
   Includes index.
   ISBN 0-531-14327-9
      1. Railroads–Juvenile literature. [1. Railroads.] I. Title.
   II. Series: Richardson, Joy. Picture science.
   TF148.R53   1994
   625.1–dc20                                   93-49731
                                                CIP  AC


 10 9 8 7 6 5 4 3 2 1


Editor: Belinda Weber
Designer: Janet Watson
Picture researcher: Sarah Moule
Illustrators: Robert and Rhoda Burns


Photographs: Chris Fairclough Colour Library 15;
Docklands Light Railway © Marcus Taylor 12;
Eye Ubiquitous © A J G Bell 11, © Michael Reed 26;
The Image Bank © Larry Gatz 23; Picturepoint cover,
title page, 28; Robert Harding Picture Library 16, 21;
Tony Stone Worldwide © Chris Kapolka 24; World
Pictures 9; ZEFA 6, © G Sommer 18.


Printed in Malaysia

# TRAINS

## Joy Richardson

**FRANKLIN WATTS**

New York • Chicago • London • Toronto • Sydney

# On track

Even before there were trains, rail tracks were used to help heavy wagons run smoothly. People or horses did the pulling.

Today there are millions of miles of railway track crisscrossing every country in the world.

Trains carry people and goods along the tracks to their destination.

# Steam trains

Steam engines pulled the
first trains along.

They work by burning coal
to heat water in the boiler.
The hot water makes steam, which
drives rods connected to the wheels.

Behind the engine there is
a tender, which carries
the coal and water supplies.

Steam engines can pull lots
of freight and passenger cars.

# Fuel supply

For one hundred years, almost
all trains ran on steam.
Now most trains use
diesel or electric power.

Diesel trains burn diesel
fuel, which comes from oil.

Electric trains use electricity
from conductor rails on the track
or from an overhead cable.

An arm on top of the train
must stay in contact with the cable
to keep the train speeding along.

# On the rails

Underneath each part of the train, there are wheels attached to a metal framework. The wheels fit onto the rail and grip the inside edge.

The rails are fixed to crossbars called sleepers.

The distance between the rails must be exactly the same all along the track. Most trains run on rails about 5 feet (1.5 m) apart.

Wheel

Rail

Sleeper

13

# Signal work

On busy lines, lots of trains
use the same stretch of track.
Signals keep the trains apart.

A red light means stop.
A green light means go.

Where the track divides,
points move the rails to keep
the train on the right track.

Displays in the signal box show
the location of each train.

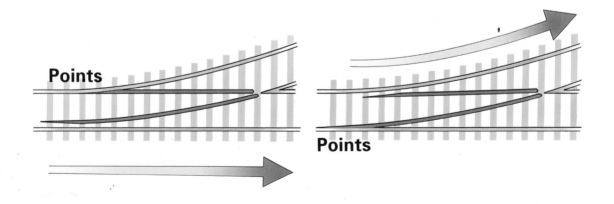

Points

Points

# Stopping the train

The driver watches the
track ahead from the cab.
There are controls for starting
and stopping the train
and for changing speed.

There are brakes on wheels
under every coach or wagon.
When the driver puts on the brakes,
all the wheels slow down.

In an emergency, passengers
can pull a handle to stop the train.

# Carrying heavy loads

Trains carry passengers and take letters and packages across the country.

Freight trains carry heavy loads from place to place.

Different kinds of wagons can be linked up to carry coal, oil tanks, tree trunks, or huge containers for delivery.

All this freight must be organized so that it can be sorted easily at the other end.

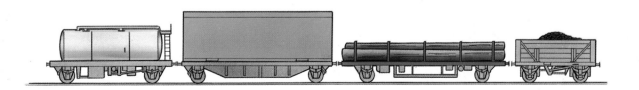

# Climbing high

Climbing is difficult for trains.

The early railroad engineers
built tunnels through hills and
viaducts over valleys to
keep the trains on a level track.

Tracks wind slowly around hillsides.
If the climb is too steep,
the train wheels will slip.

Special mountain railroads
have a cogwheel that grips a
toothed rail in the middle of the track.

# Under the ground

Underground trains carry
people across busy cities.

They travel through tunnels
bored deep under the streets.

The trains run on electricity
from a conductor rail on the track.

Electronic systems control the
signals and make trains stop.
The doors open automatically.

Some underground trains could
operate without a driver.

# High-speed trains

New high-speed trains can
carry people from city to city
almost as fast as an airplane.

Electricity comes from overhead cables.
There are electric motors under
each car to help drive the wheels.

The fastest trains run on special
straight tracks with no signals.

High-speed trains are
streamlined like airplanes,
which helps to stop the rush of
air slowing them down.

# Changing trains

Lightweight railroads are being built
to carry passengers speedily
over short distances.

Monorail trains run along
or hang from a single rail.
They can carry people
high above the ground.

Maglevs are a new type
of train without rails.
Magnets lift the train and make
it glide along above the track.

Trains are changing fast.

# Train facts

The fastest train is the French high-speed train that reached over 310 miles per hour (500 km/h).

The fastest thing on rails was a rocket-powered sledge that reached almost 6,215 miles per hour (10,000 km/h). There was no one in it.

There are narrow-gauge railroads in Britain with rails as little as 10 inches (26 cm) apart.

# Index